GREAT ILLUSTRATED CLASSICS

KING ARTHUR
AND THE
KNIGHTS OF
THE ROUND TABLE
HOWARD PYLE

Adapted by **Joshua E. Hanft**

Illustrations by **Pablo Marcos Studio**

BARONET BOOKS, New York, New York

GREAT ILLUSTRATED CLASSICS

edited by
Joshua Hanft

Contents

About the Author

Howard Pyle was born in Wilmington, Delaware in 1853. After he finished high school, he went to an art school and then worked in his father's leather shop. Soon he returned to the work he loved best—illustrations—and opened his own school for young artists.

Pyle liked to create special worlds where anything could happen. He called them "islands of fantasy or imagination." Sometimes he used his brush to capture these worlds in pictures, and sometimes his pen to write the stories himself. These stories include pirate adventures on the high seas, vivid tales of American colonial life, and legends of the knights in the days of chivalry.

In *King Arthur and the Knights of the Round Table,* Pyle invites us into one of his many fantasy lands. He spent seven years researching, illustrating and compiling four volumes on the legends of King Arthur. He studied legends that were written in Old English, Welsh, French, and German.

Howard Pyle gathered these old tales and retold them in his own way, writing them down so anyone could open a book anytime, anyplace, and step into the magical fantasy worlds he loved best.

The Noble Old King

CHAPTER 1

The Secret Birth

In ancient days there lived a noble king named Uther-Pendragon. He gathered together many brave knights, defeated all his enemies, and became overlord of all England.

In his struggle against his enemies, Uther-Pendragon was aided by two great counselors. One of these men was a powerful enchanter and prophet known to all as Merlin the Wise; the other was a renowned knight called Sir Ulfius. With the aid and assistance of Merlin and Ulfius, Uther-Pendragon made peace in the realm he ruled with justice and mercy.

After a number of years, Uther-Pendragon took

as his wife a beautiful, gentle queen named Igraine. Igraine was the widow of Gerlois, the Duke of Tintegal. Before she married Uther-Pendragon she had already borne two daughters, Margaise and Morgana le Fay.

Igraine brought her daughters with her to the court of Uther-Pendragon. The king treated them as if they were his own children, and arranged noble marriages for them. Yet Uther-Pendragon worried who would succeed him as king.

After a time Queen Igraine knew she would have a baby. Uther-Pendragon rejoiced and planned to celebrate the birth of his child. Then Merlin came to him in secret and counseled him to tell no one about the baby.

"My lord," Merlin advised, "this must be a secret birth. When the child is born, I will tell you more."

Uther-Pendragon had learned to always follow Merlin's words, and his heart was sorely troubled. At last the child was born, a beautiful baby boy, of

Igraine and Her Daughters

great size and strength. The proud mother and father wrapped him in warm clothes and lay him in a cradle of gold and ultramarine—the cradle of a future king.

When Merlin came to the king, his face was clouded with worry, his eyes sad and misty.

"My lord, you know the spirit of prophecy is strong within me. I can foresee that you shall shortly fall sick with a great fever and will not live. Your child will be defenseless, and enemies will either kill or imprison him. Please give me the child. Sir Ulfius and I will hide him and find a place where he can grow to manhood safe from the dangers that beset him."

"Merlin," replied Uther-Pendragon, "as far as my death is concerned—when my time comes to die, I believe God will give me grace to meet my end with cheerfulness and strength; for, certainly all men must die, whether they be kings or slaves.

"But on the matter of the child, if your prophecy is true, his danger is great. Convey him

Merlin Warns the King.

to safety and watch over him. For this baby is the most precious inheritance this land shall ever know."

Merlin did as he was advised. In the middle of the night he and Sir Ulfius took the child away, but no one knew where. A few months later, Uther-Pendragon was seized with a sickness, as Merlin had foretold. The brave king faced his death with the strength and courage he had shown throughout his life.

After Uther-Pendragon died, it was as Merlin predicted. The realm fell into great disorder. Lesser kings contended with each other to become overlord. Wicked knights and barons captured travelers and held them for ransom. Those who could not pay were killed. Injustice ruled. Knight fought knight in deadly battle, not for honor, but for gain.

People wished for a new king to rule. The land groaned with the terrible trouble that lay upon it.

Not for Honor, But for Gain

"Use Your Mighty Wisdom!"

CHAPTER 2

The Sword in the Stone

Thus passed nearly eighteen years of great affliction. Then one day, the Archbishop of Canterbury summoned Merlin.

"Merlin, people say that you are the wisest man in all the world. Can you find some way to heal the problems that afflict this realm? Use your mighty wisdom to help our people find a king so that we may enjoy happiness as we did in the days of Uther-Pendragon."

"My lord Archbishop," Merlin answered, "the spirit of prophecy moves me now to say that this country shall soon have a king who will be even wiser and greater and more worthy of praise than Uther-Pendragon. And he shall bring order and peace where there is now disorder and war. Moreover, I may tell you that this king shall be of Uther-Pendragon's own blood-royal."

The archbishop asked Merlin how they would know the true king from those who only claimed to be rightful king.

"My lord," responded Merlin, "I will use my magic to create an obstacle, which, if any man shall solve it, all the world will know that man is the rightful king and overlord of this realm."

The archbishop readily agreed. Merlin made a huge marble stone suddenly appear in an open place before the cathedral. Under the marble was a stone and into the stone was thrust a great naked sword, the most wonderful sword that any man had ever seen, extraordinarily bright and glittering. The hilt was gold, carved and inlaid with beautiful precious stones that flashed in the sunlight. Near the sword was written in letters of

The Sword in the Stone

gold:

WHOSO PULLETH OUT THIS SWORD FROM THE STONE THAT SAME IS RIGHT-WISE KING-BORN OF ENGLAND.

Many people came to gaze on the sword and marvel at its beauty. When Merlin had accomplished this, the archbishop announced that every man who aspired to be king must try to pull the sword from the stone; whoever succeeded would be the rightful king of England.

When the mandate of the archbishop went forth, all the people of the realm stirred in wonder.

"Who shall be our king?" they asked. Many thought it would be King Lot of Orkney or King Urien of Gore, for these were the husbands of Queen Igraine's daughters. Some thought it would be King Leodegrance, father of the beautiful Guenivere. No one knew, but all eagerly awaited the outcome.

Then it seemed as if the entire world was on its way to London, for the highways and byways were filled with kings and lords, knights and

The Archbishop's Mandate

ladies, esquires and pages. Every inn and castle was filled with travellers. People pitched tents and pavilions along the wayside when accommodation indoors could not be found.

When the archbishop beheld the multitudes that were assembling, he said to Merlin, "Indeed it would be amazing if among all these great knights and kings, we should not find someone to be king of the realm."

Merlin smiled and said, "Do not be surprised if among all these famous kings and knights not one is found worthy. But also do not be surprised if among those who are entirely unknown, one shall prove himself to be the rightful heir to the throne."

On the Road to London

Sir Ector and Sir Kay

CHAPTER 3

A Young Boy's Miracle

Among those who assembled in London at this time was Sir Ector of Bonmaison. This noble and excellent knight was held in great regard by all who knew him. He had two sons, the elder, Sir Kay, a young knight of great valor, was already well renowned in the courts of chivalry for his worthy deeds. The younger son was Arthur, who had just turned eighteen. He served as Sir Kay's esquire-at-arms.

Sir Ector, being of noble blood, took up the archbishop's decree. He hoped Sir Kay could be the one to pull the sword from the stone. So Sir Ector, Sir Kay, and Arthur came to London and set up a pavilion emblazoned with the emblem of their house, a black gryphon upon a field of green. Outside London, many pavilions of many noble houses filled the sky with a multitude of brightly colored pennants and banners.

The Archbishop of Canterbury, seeing so many lords and knights assembled for the great adventure of the sword and the stone, decided to hold a tournament of men-at-arms to see who was the most noble and accomplished knight.

Now when Sir Kay heard of this tournament, he asked his father's permission to enter. With his father's approval, Sir Kay, being of noble blood, was admitted to the lists. He chose his younger brother, Arthur, to be his esquire-at-arms and to carry his spear and pennant before him into the field of battle. Arthur was exceedingly happy at the great honor he had been given.

Soon the day of the tournament arrived. More than twenty thousand lords and ladies came to see the proud young men do battle. The contesting

An Honor for Young Arthur

knights were divided into two camps, at the north and south end of the field. Sir Kay attached himself to the north end, which had fewer knights, but included Sir Bedivere and others known for their great strength and valor.

The two companies met, one against the other, in the midst of the field. The roar of breaking lances was so terrible that several ladies swooned with terror as the air was filled with the splinters of shattered wood. In this famous assault many knights were overthrown, and many were trampled beneath the hoofs of the rushing horses. Some champions tried to raise themselves from the ground, but were too weakened. Attendants and esquires ran to their leaders, replacing broken spears and ruined armor.

In this assault Sir Kay conducted himself with such credit that no knight did better. He fought knight after knight and conquered all. Midway in battle he encountered Sir Balmorgineas, who called out to him, "Ho! Sir Knight of the black gryphon, turn this way and do battle with me!"

No Knight Did Better than Sir Kay.

Sir Kay, full of the spirit of youth, turned with eagerness and fury to battle. With his sword he struck Sir Balmorgineas a fierce blow on the top of his helmet. But Sir Kay's sword-blade snapped from the ferocity of the blow, and he was left without any weapon and at the mercy of Sir Balmorgineas. Three of his companions in arms, perceiving his peril, protected him and brought him to the far end of the field and safety.

When he reached the barrier, young Arthur came running to him with a goblet of spiced wine. Sir Kay drank quickly and called out, "Run as fast as you can to our pavilion, and fetch me a new sword."

Off ran Arthur. But when he got to Sir Ector's pavilion he found no one. All had gone to the tournament, nor could he find a sword. Then Arthur thought of the sword he had seen thrust into the stone near the cathedral. Such a sword would suit his brother's purpose very well, he thought.

There was no guard near the sword, so Arthur leapt upon the rock and laid his hands on the hilt.

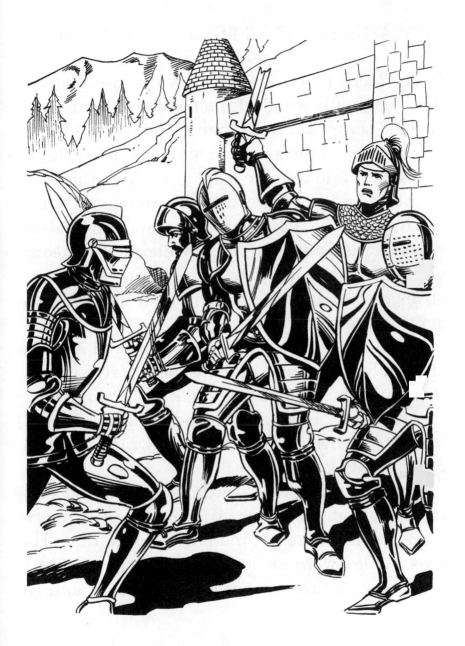

No Weapon!

In one quick movement he drew the sword out of the stone with wonderful smoothness and ease. He held the sword in his hand, and it was his!

He wrapped the sword in his cloak, for it shone so brightly, and then he leapt down from the marble block and ran toward the tournament. When Sir Kay beheld the sword he knew immediately what it was and stood for a while, like someone who had been turned to stone. Then, in a very strange voice he asked, "Arthur, where did you get this sword?"

"I will tell the entire truth," answered Arthur, "I could find no sword in our father's pavilion, so I thought of the sword I saw stuck in the stone near the cathedral. I went there and pulled on it, and it came out with marvelous ease. I wrapped it and brought it to you."

Sir Kay's thoughts turned inward, and he said to himself: my brother Arthur is hardly more than a child, a very innocent child at that. He does not know what he has done. Why should I myself not lay claim to this achievement and so

The Sword Was His!

obtain the glory it signifies?

"Arthur," said Sir Kay, "Give the sword and the cloak to me, and tell no man what happened. Go to our father where he sits at the lists and tell him to come to me immediately."

Arthur did as Sir Kay commanded him, confused as to why his brother seemed so disturbed. Young Arthur had no idea of the great deed he had performed.

"Give the Sword to Me."

Something Extraordinary Must Have Happened.

CHAPTER 4

A New King

Arthur ran to his father, as his brother had ordered.

"Sire, my brother, Sir Kay, has sent me here and bids you come to him right away," he told Sir Ector. "I think something extraordinary must have happened."

Sir Ector marvelled at what could cause Sir Kay to quit the battle and summon him at such a time. So he arose from the lists, and with Arthur by his side made his way to their pavilion. There he saw Sir Kay's face was white and that his eyes shone feverishly.

"My son, what is wrong?" cried out Sir Ector.

"Sire, here is a wonderful thing!" answered Sir Kay, and without another word unwrapped the cloak that hid the sword. Sir Ector immediately knew the sword and where it came from. He was astonished and didn't know what to do at first. Then he found his voice and asked, "What is this that my eyes behold?"

To this Sir Kay replied, "I have that sword that stood embedded in the stone. Tell me, I demand, what glory it may mean for me?"

But Sir Ector asked sharply, "How did you come by that sword?"

Sir Kay thought a while before he answered. "I broke my sword in battle and then I found this one to take its place."

Sir Ector was astonished and could not believe what his ears had heard. "If you drew the sword from the anvil, then you are rightful King of England. For the saying near the sword proclaims this. But if you did indeed draw forth the sword, then you can thrust it back into the place it came from."

"What is this that My Eyes Behold?"

At these words, Sir Kay was deeply troubled. "How can one put the sword back? The stone is like solid iron. It would take a miracle to thrust the sword back in."

"No greater miracle than to take out the sword in the first place," his father answered.

Sir Kay took comfort in knowing that his younger brother had already performed this miracle. "If young Arthur was able to do it, so can I," he said to himself.

So they wrapped the sword in the cloak and together Sir Ector, Sir Kay, and Arthur returned to the cathedral. Sir Kay looked at the stone, which had become smooth again, and said to himself, "What man is there in life who could thrust a sword-blade into a solid stone like iron? Still I must try."

But it was impossible. He could not pierce the iron at all. After he tried and tried in vain, he called out to his father, "Sire, no man can perform this miracle."

But Sir Ector suspiciously replied, "How then

It Would Take A Miracle.

was it possible for you to draw the sword out?"

"My father, may I speak?" young Arthur lifted his voice and asked.

And Sir Ector said, "Speak, my son."

"I would like to try to return the sword to the stone, since I was the one who took it out." Arthur said. Arthur took the sword from his brother, Sir Kay, and leapt upon the marble stone. He set the point of the sword upon the stone and the sword penetrated as smoothly as if it were butter. He drew the sword out again, and then once more put it back.

When Sir Ector saw what Arthur had done, he cried out in a loud voice, "Lord! Lord! My eyes have beheld a miracle." And when Arthur leapt down from the marble block Sir Ector knelt down before him.

When Arthur saw his father kneel, he cried aloud, "My Father! My Father! Why do you kneel before me?"

"I am not your father. Now it is made clear that you are of a very exalted race and the blood of

As If it were Butter

kings flows in your veins."

All the while Sir Kay stood by like one en-tranced. Finally he said to himself, "What is this? Is my brother a king?"

Then Sir Ector spoke again. "The time is come, Arthur, for you to know the true circumstances of your life which before now have been hidden from you.

"Eighteen years ago, during the last year of the reign of Uther-Pendragon, a wise man known as Merlin came to me, bearing the King,s signet ring. He commanded me by virtue of that ring to be in a certain place at a certain time near Uther-Pendragon's castle.

"He warned me to tell nobody of these com-mands, and I kept his counsel. I went to the place he had ordered, and two men came.to me, Merlin himself and Sir Ulfius. Merlin bore in his arms a scarlet mantle of the finest texture. He opened the folds of the mantle and there lay a child in swaddling clothes. You were that child.

"Merlin commanded me to take that child and

"I Am Not Your Father."

raise him as if he were my own. And he said the child was to be named Arthur, and no one in the world was to know where I had gotten him. From that day forward I have done as he commanded. Not until now have I ever really suspected who was your true father, though I believed you to be of very kingly blood. But now I believe you are the son of Uther-Pendragon himself!"

At these words, Arthur cried aloud, "No! No! No!"

"Why are you sad, my king?" asked Sir Ector, kneeling once more to the young boy.

"Because I have lost my father," answered Arthur. "I would rather have my father back than be a king!"

Now, as these things passed, there came to that place two men, very tall and of a wonderfully noble and haughty appearance. And when they came closer, Sir Ector realized that they were Sir Ulfius and Merlin.

"What cheer?" asked Merlin.

"Here is news of a wonderful sort," replied Sir

"Merlin Commanded Me."

Ector, "for here is the child you gave me eighteen years ago."

"I know," said Merlin. "In him lie the hopes of all England. He shall become the greatest and most famous king that ever lived. Many knights of extraordinary excellence shall gather round him. And men shall tell of their marvelous deeds as long as the land shall continue. Rejoice, Sir Ector, for a great new age is dawning!"

A Great New Age is Dawning.

Kings and Dukes Would Try to Lift the Sword

CHAPTER 5

The King Revealed

Christmas morning arrived. Thousands came to see all the kings and dukes attempt to lift the sword from the stone. The archbishop sat upon the high throne, all his court of clerks and knights gathered about him.

Nineteen kings and sixteen dukes of royal lineage were to try to lift the sword from the stone. The atmosphere was filled with excitement and anticipation.

First to make trial of the sword was King Lot of Orkney, son-in-law of Uther-Pendragon. He climbed the marble rock, saluted the arch-bishop and bent over the sword. But try as he might, he was unable to move the sword, even slightly. Three times he tried, but each time came no closer. Finally he gave up.

King Urien, Uther-Pendragon's other son-in-law, tried next. But neither did he succeed. Nor did King Fion of Scotland, or King Mark of Cornwall or King Leodegrance of Cameliard or King Pellinore. Try as they might, no king nor duke was able to move the sword. Some were angry, others ashamed.

When all the kings and dukes had failed, the crowd began to whisper: "How is this? If all those kings and dukes of exalted estate have failed to achieve this, who then can succeed?"

So too the kings began to talk among themselves. Then they approached the archbishop:

"Sir, here have all the kings and dukes of the realm striven before you to lift the sword from the stone and none have succeeded. Perhaps the enchanter Merlin has set this adventure only to bring shame and discredit upon us. For who in the world could draw a sword out of an iron

All the Kings and Dukes Had Failed.

stone? It is impossible. We ask you to choose from your great wisdom one of us to become overlord."

"Have faith," the archbishop called out, "for surely Merlin will explain this to us all."

Merlin had bidden Arthur, Sir Kay and Sir Ector to keep hidden until he was ready for them. Now Merlin and Sir Ulfius walked into Sir Ector's pavilion and spoke.

"Arise, Arthur," Merlin called. "It is time for you to show the world the miracle you showed us."

Arthur did as Merlin asked and came forth from the pavilion dressed in flame-colored embroidered robes.

They went to the cathedral and the great marble rock. The crowds let them pass as people asked, "Who are these with the enchanter Merlin and Sir Ulfius?" Merlin said no word to anyone, but brought Arthur directly to where the archbishop sat.

The archbishop arose and asked, "Merlin, who are these you bring with you and what is their

"Merlin Will Explain This."

business here?"

"Here is one to try to pull the sword from the stone," he answered, and called Arthur forward.

"Merlin, by what right does this young man come forward?" asked one of the angry kings.

"By the best right there is," shouted Merlin, "for he who stands before you is the true son of Uther-Pendragon!"

"But Uther-Pendragon had no children," cried out the archbishop.

"Not so," answered Merlin and told the crowd of Arthur,s secret birth.

"All that Merlin has spoken is true," rang out the voices of Sir Ector and Sir Ulfius. "Let the boy show you."

Then Arthur laid his hands upon the sword, lifted it out of the stone and swung it around his head three times. Then he placed it back in the stone. Now when the people who were congregated at that place beheld it, they shouted so loud that it was as though the whole earth rocked and trembled.

"Let the Boy Show You."

And while they shouted, Arthur took hold of the sword, lifted it from the stone and once more swung it about his head three times. Then he placed it back in the stone, picked it up yet again and repeated it for the third time.

All the kings and dukes were filled with great amazement that a young man was able to perform what they had failed to do. Most were willing to acknowledge Arthur as the true king. Some, like King Pellinore, felt bitter in their hearts, and vowed to fight the new king.

The archbishop proclaimed Arthur king of all England. The crowd gave another great shout. As Arthur departed, the crowds followed after him, hoping to get near him or touch his clothes. Arthur was uplifted with great joy and gladness, so that his soul took wing and flew like a bird into the sky.

The Archbishop Proclaimed Arthur King.

Home of the Black Knight

CHAPTER 6

King Arthur and the Black Knight

Word came to King Arthur in his court at Camelot of an evil knight in black armor who lived in a deep forest and attacked all who trespassed near his lonely castle. To the young king, defeating the black knight in battle would be a worthy deed. So in his armor, together with Merlin, he set out for the forest.

After a while they saw a violent stream of water that rushed through a dark and dismal glen. Over the water was a stone bridge and beyond the bridge a tall, dark, forbidding castle. Upon the bridge hung a black shield beneath which was written: —

WHOSO SMITETH THIS SHIELD
DOETH SO AT HIS PERIL.

On an apple tree nearby hung the shields of many knights who had attacked the black knight and had been defeated.

"This must indeed be a powerful knight who has overthrown so many other knights. For indeed there must be a hundred shields hanging from yonder tree!" said King Arthur.

"May you be happy," replied Merlin, "if your own shield does not hang there before the day is over."

"That," said Arthur, "will be as God wills, for I have a greater mind than ever to try my power against this knight." He seized his mace and struck the black shield a resounding blow that echoed throughout the forest.

In answer, the gates of the castle opened and out came a huge knight clad in armor black as ebony. He rode with much pride, as became a champion who had never been overcome in battle.

WHOSO SMITETH THIS
SHIELD DOETH SO
AT HIS PERIL

Shields of the Defeated Knights

"Why did you dare to smite my shield? For your discourtesy I shall take your shield and hang it upon yonder apple tree where you behold the shields of others who dared to fight me," he called out.

"Know this, unkind knight," returned King Arthur, "I have come here to redeem with my person all those shields that hang upon the tree. You shall yield *your* shield to me!"

Each got ready his spear and shield. They shouted to their war-horses and drove toward each other. Those two noble steeds rushed like lightning, coursing the ground with violent speed. The two fierce riders crashed together like thunderbolts, and their spears burst into splinters.

They tried again with new spears, but once again the spears shattered, and once again neither rider was able to unhorse his enemy. Then they tried for the third time. King Arthur's spear burst into splinters, but the spear of the black knight held steady and pierced through the center of King Arthur's shield. The straps of the

"Why Did You Dare Smite My Shield?"

King's saddle burst from the violence of the blow, and his horse was cast violently backward. King Arthur jumped off his horse with knightly grace and landed on his feet. The blow he received was so great, however, that for a time he lost his senses, and everything whirled before his eyes.

When he had recovered, he cried out, "Come down, black knight, and fight me on foot and with your sword!"

"That I will not do," replied the black knight. "I have overthrown you. You must deliver your shield to me."

King Arthur grabbed the bridle-rein of the black knight,s horse and thrust it back so roughly that the black knight had to jump off his horse to keep from being overthrown.

And now each man drew his sword and rushed together like two bulls in battle. They struck and parried, and struck again. The force of their blows echoed throughout the forest. Whole chunks of armor were hewn from their bodies and each received many serious wounds. At last King

His Horse Was Cast Violently Backward.

Arthur struck such a blow with his sword that the black knight groaned and staggered and ran about in circles. But the force of the blow had broken King Arthur's own sword so he was unable to complete his victory. Presently the black knight recovered and taking his own sword into both hands struck King Arthur on his helmet with so powerful a stroke that it broke the helmet and seriously wounded the king.

Seeing him so seriously injured, the black knight called for Arthur to surrender. Arthur would not yield, but lifted himself up by his enemy's sword-belt. Then he circled the black knight with both arms, placed his knee behind the knight's thigh and cast him backward upon the ground. With that fall the black knight lost consciousness. Arthur straightway unlaced the knight's helmet and knew that it was none other than King Pellinore, his old enemy.

"Ha! Pellinore, is it you? Now yield to me, for you are at my mercy!" Arthur cried. He drew a small dagger and held it at his neck.

The Black Knight Groaned and Staggered.

By now Pellinore had recovered from his fall. Seeing how weak his enemy was from the head wound he had given him, he forced the dagger away and heaved King Arthur to the ground. Pellinore picked up the dagger and made ready to kill his opponent.

"Stay, Pellinore," called out the voice of Merlin. "Hold your sacrilegious hand! For he who lies beneath you is none other than Arthur, king of all this realm!"

"Say you so, old man," shouted out Pellinore, "then you yourself have doomed him! For Arthur is my enemy who has taken my land, my kingship, and my glory."

Merlin lifted up his staff and hit Pellinore across the shoulders. Pellinore immediately fell down as one struck dead.

Arthur beheld his enemy lying as though dead and cried out, "Merlin, what have you done? With your magic you have killed someone who had bested me in fair combat!"

"Not so," said Merlin. "He is but asleep. You are

Pellinore, His Old Enemy!

much closer to death. Without aid, you will die shortly."

So saying, Merlin slung the wounded Arthur across his horse and led him deep into the forest. He brought Arthur to a holy hermit skilled in treating wounds. He helped keep Arthur alive. But the young king was very weak and his recovery was in doubt.

On the next day, there came a great noise. It happened that the Lady Guinevere of Cameliard, together with her court, had decided to make a pilgrimage to see the holy hermit. In front of the hermitage, Guinevere saw King Arthur's milk-white war-horse tethered to a tree.

"Whose noble horse is that?" she asked Merlin, who stood nearby.

"Alas, it belongs to a knight who lies seriously wounded inside," Merlin answered. "He is near death."

"Pity of heaven!" cried the Lady Guinevere, "may I see the wounded knight?" So Merlin brought her into the hermit's cell. She did not

"Whose Noble Horse is That?"

know it was King Arthur, but thought she had never beheld so noble a knight in all her life. Arthur, in his weakened state, thought an angel from Paradise had descended to visit him.

Guinevere had in her court a skilled doctor who tended Arthur's wounds. When the lady and her court departed, Arthur was almost entirely healed.

This was the first time that Arthur ever beheld that beautiful lady, Guinevere of Cameliard. From that time on she was always in his thoughts, and he pledged that he would serve this lady as faithfully as ever a good knight may serve his chosen lady.

"May I See the Wounded Knight?"

"I Might Have Conquered That Knight."

CHAPTER 7

Excaliber

Despite the wounds he had received from King Pellinore, Arthur longed to try his foe in combat once more.

"For had my sword not broken," he told Merlin, "I might have conquered that knight. I will challenge him once again."

"But you have no sword and no spear, my lord," Merlin reminded him. "How can you undertake this adventure without due preparation?"

"Had I no better weapon than an oaken cudgel, yet I would take on King Pellinore once more," King Arthur said.

Seeing how fixed King Arthur was in his

purpose, Merlin told him the legend of Excaliber.

"Near here is the Forest of Adventure. No knight may enter there without an adventure befalling him. Right in the middle of this forest of enchantment is a beautiful wide lake. In the center of that lake is a woman's arm, clad in white samite, the hand holding a sword of such exceeding excellence and beauty that no eye has ever beheld its like. The name of this sword is Excaliber.

"Several knights have seen this sword and tried to get it. But not one has been able to reach it, and many have lost their lives trying. For when any man draws near it, either he sinks into the lake or the arm is withdrawn completely. Perhaps you can be the man who gains the glory of capturing the sword."

"Lead me to this enchanted land," ordered the king. And Merlin did so.

When they entered the enchanted woodlands, they beheld a white doe with a golden collar. They followed her to an opening in the woods of soft sweet grass. A bower was set with a table of

The Forest of Adventure

refreshments, white bread, meats, and wine. At the door stood a page boy clad all in green.

"Ho! King Arthur! Welcome to this place!" he called out to them. "Dismount and partake of the bounty."

Arthur hesitated, astonished that this page deep in the forest knew his name. But Merlin assured him that it was a good omen, and they ate and refreshed themselves. After, they came upon a meadow filled with the most beautiful flowers they had ever seen. This was a land where the air was so radiant and so bright it appeared to be spun of gold. Bright colored birds sung sweetly in the sky. And midway in the meadow was a beautiful wide lake.

At the edge of the lake was what Merlin had foretold. In the midst of the water was the fair and beautiful arm, clad in white samite. The hand held a sword of marvelous workmanship, the hilt crusted with precious jewels and the blade so bright, it reflected like a shooting star.

King Arthur sat upon his war-horse and gazed

"Ho, King Arthur! Welcome!"

at the sword. He wondered how he could reach it, for the lake was wide and deep. As he sat pondering, he suddenly saw a strange lady approaching through the tall flowers. He quickly dismounted and went forward to meet her.

As he grew closer he saw that she was very beautiful, with perfectly black eyes as bright and glistening as two jewels set in ivory. She was all in green, and around her neck hung a beautiful necklace of opals and emeralds set in cunningly wrought gold. King Arthur knelt before her and said, "Lady, I see that you are no mortal damsel, but are certainly a fairy. And I have entered an enchanted land."

The lady replied: "King Arthur, you speak truly, for I am indeed. My name is Nymue, and I am leader of the Ladies of the Lake. And know that what you behold is not really a lake, but a meadow filled with flowers, in the midst of which stands a white castle. To prevent mortal eyes from seeing our home, my sisters and I have made appear a lake through which no man may pass."

The Sword in the Lake

"Lady," said King Arthur, "I fear that in coming here I intrude upon the solitude of your dwelling place."

"Nay, not so, King Arthur," said the Lady of the Lake, "for in truth you are very welcome. I have a great friendliness for you and the noble knights of your court. What brings you to this land?"

King Arthur told her of his battle, his need for a new sword, and how he wanted Excaliber. "That sword is no easy thing to achieve," she answered. "No man may win Excaliber unless he is without fear and beyond reproach."

"Alas, Lady," said King Arthur, "I may not lack in courage but there are things for which I do reproach myself. I will still attempt to win the sword. What is the best way?"

Then the Lady of the Lake drew a whistle to her lips. Straight away a boat carved of brass, swift as a swan, sped from the middle of the lake to the shore. The Lady of the Lake bade King Arthur enter the boat, and immediately King Arthur felt the boat float swiftly toward the

The Lady of the Lake

sword. He reached forward and took the sword in his hand, and the arm disappeared beneath the water. Then the king's heart swelled with joy, for Excaliber was a hundred times more beautiful than he had imagined.

The boat quickly carried him back and he gave the Lady of the Lake great thanks for all that she had done to help him. King Arthur, with Merlin, rode away, rejoicing at having for his own the most beautiful and famous sword in all the world.

The Most Famous Sword in the World

"No Magic Shall Determine Right."

CHAPTER 8

To Battle Again!

About noontime the next day they reached the valley of the black knight. All looked as it did before: the gloomy castle, the apple-tree covered with shields, the bridge where the black shield was hung.

"Now, Merlin," said King Arthur, "I strictly forbid you to enter this quarrel. No magic shall determine right. It shall be between bold knights defending their valor."

The king rode forth upon the bridge, and once again struck the sable shield with all his might. Immediately the gates of the castle opened and the black knight rode forth, equipped for the encounter. As he came to the bridge-head, King Arthur spoke to him.

"Sir Pellinore, we now know one another well, and each has his own opinions as to the causes of our quarrel. You feel that I have taken away your kingly estate and have driven you to this forest. I feel that you have set yourself here to do injury and affront to the knights in my kingdom. Let us fight, man to man, until one of us has conquered the other."

King Pellinore bowed his head in agreement and each combatant rode off a ways, then wheeled to confront the other. Once again their spears burst into splinters, but neither was able to unseat the other. Then each knight jumped off his horse and drew his sword. But now, having Excaliber to aid him, King Arthur soon overcame his enemy. For he gave King Pellinore several wounds, yet received none himself. And at last King Arthur delivered so bold a stroke that King Pellinore felt his whole body go numb. He dropped his sword and shield and sank upon his

Their Spears Burst Into Splinters.

knees. Then he called upon King Arthur to have mercy, saying, "Spare my life and I will yield to you."

King Arthur answered, "I will spare you and do more than that. For now that you have yielded yourself to me, I will restore you to your power and your land. I bear you no ill-will, Pellinore. But I can brook no rebels in this realm. As God judges me, I do rule singly in this kingdom. He who is against me is against my people, and he who is against my people is against me. As a pledge of your good faith, you will send to me your two sons, Sir Aglaval and Sir Lamorack, to serve as knights in my court."

Then King Arthur carried King Pellinore back to his castle and made sure his wounds were taken care of. And peace and harmony were for a time brought to the kingdom.

Now as King Arthur and Merlin rode back to the court, Arthur was filled with happiness over both his victory and his new sword. After a time Merlin questioned the king.

"I Brook No Rebels in this Realm."

"Arthur, which would you rather have, Excaliber, or the sheath which holds it?"

To which Arthur replied, "Why, ten thousand times would I rather have Excaliber than its sheath."

"In this you are wrong, my lord," said Merlin, "for let me tell you that though Excaliber is so sharp that it can cut either a feather or an iron bar in two, yet its sheath is so magical that he who wears it can suffer no wound in battle, nor lose a single drop of blood. For as you saw in your last battle with King Pellinore you suffered no wounds at all."

Then King Arthur looked angrily at Merlin, for all the pleasure he had received from defeating King Pellinore had disappeared.

"Merlin, I do declare that you have taken from me the entire glory of that battle. For what credit may fall to any knight who fights his enemy by means of enchantment? I have half a mind to take this glorious sword back to the magic lake and cast it where it belongs."

"Rather Would I Have Excaliber!"

"My lord," said Merlin, "assuredly you are right in what you say. But bear in mind that you are not an ordinary knight, but a king. Your life belongs not to you but to your people. You have no right to imperil it, but should do all that lies in your power to preserve it. Keep the sword so that it may safeguard your life."

King Arthur meditated for a while and realized Merlin was right. But he decided to use the sword only in serious battle. Thereafter he did no battle in sport except with a lance and on horseback.

So King Arthur treasured Excaliber and the sword remained with him for all of his life. The sword became the most famous of any that was ever seen in all the courts of chivalry.

"Your Life Belongs to Your People."

A Herald-Messenger from the West-Country

CHAPTER 9

The Magic Cap

One day as King Arthur feasted in Camelot, surrounded by his knights, a messenger-herald arrived from the west-country. The messenger was from King Leodegrance of Cameliard, one of his first allies. He informed Arthur that their mutual enemy King Ryence of North Wales had demanded from King Leodegrance the return of lands that bordered their countries. Ryence had also demanded that King Leodegrance deliver his daughter, Lady Guinevere to his nephew, Duke Mordaunt of North Umber. Now Duke Mordaunt, though a mighty warrior, was of evil appearance and violent in temper. But King Leodegrance had no army to defend his kingdom so he called upon Arthur for aid.

When Arthur heard this news he became furious. He rose from the chair where he sat and went into an inner room of the castle to be by himself. From the moment he had set his eyes on the Lady Guinevere in the hermit's hut, he had considered her the fairest lady on earth, and the thought of her marriage to the ugly and evil Duke Mordaunt drove him to a frenzy.

Then, after a while he commanded that Merlin, Sir Ulfius, and Sir Kay should come to him. He talked with them for a long time, bidding Merlin to ready himself for a journey with him. He told Sir Ulfius and Sir Kay to gather together a large army of chosen knights and bring them to his castle at Tintagolon near the borders of North Wales and Cameliard.

They traveled all the next day to Tintagolon without adventure or misadventure of any sort. Arthur was received with great rejoicing, for

He Considered Her the Fairest Lady on Earth.

wherever the king went, the people loved him dearly.

The next morning Arthur and Merlin walked in the woods and Arthur opened his mind to Merlin.

"Merlin, I do believe the Lady Guinevere is the fairest lady in all of the world, and my heart is filled with love for her. I think of her continually, whether I am eating, drinking, walking or sitting still. The thought of another man taking her for his wife drives me mad. I will not have it!

"Now I know you are cunning in the arts of magic that may change a man's appearance so that even those who know him best can not recognize him. I desire you to disguise me so that I may go, unknown of any man, to Cameliard so that I may see the Lady Guinevere every day. For I desire to behold her in such a way that she may not know of my regard. So too, this way I will see

"You Are Cunning in the Arts of Magic."

the perils that surround my good friend, King Leodegrance."

Upon returning to the castle, Merlin came to the king and gave him a little cap. The cap was a magic one, for as the king set it upon his head, in that instant he assumed the appearance of a rude and rustic fellow from the countryside. The king ordered a jerkin of rough fabric be brought to him and with this he covered his royal and knightly clothes and hid the golden collar that he always wore around his neck. Then setting the cap upon his head, he assumed his disguise. Entirely unrecognizable, he left Tintagolon and took his way on foot to the town of Cameliard that lay at the base of the castle.

By the end of the day he came to the castle itself, and in the guise of a poor peasant from the countryside, no man in the world knew who he was. At the castle, he made inquiries for the head gardener. He asked him for work in that part of the garden near where he knew dwelled the Lady

Looking Like a Country Fellow

Guinevere. The gardener looked upon him and saw a tall and well-framed lad and hired him immediately.

And thus it was that King Arthur became a gardener's boy at Cameliard.

King Arthur Became a Gardener's Boy.

Lady Guinevere Came Every Day to Walk There.

CHAPTER 10

The Gardener's Boy

King Arthur was glad to be in the garden, for in this pleasant summer season the Lady Guinevere came every day to walk there. For a whole week King Arthur enjoyed being a simple worker without bearing the burden of kingship, and he was near the lady of his heart.

Early one morning when the weather was rather warm, one of Guinevere's attendants, the Lady Mellicene, glanced out the window that overlooked the rose garden beneath Guinevere's bower. Below her she saw the figure of a noble knight bathing himself in the fountain. His reddish-gold hair glistened in the sun, and around his neck hung a golden collar of marvelous beauty.

Quickly, Mellicene ran down the turret stairs to find out how this noble knight had stolen into the garden. But King Arthur, hearing her coming, speedily set his magic cap on his head. When the damsel reached the fountain, only the gardener's boy was there.

"Who are you?" demanded the lady. "Why do you sit by the fountain, and did you see the noble knight who was bathing here?"

"I am the gardener's lad," Arthur replied, "and there has been no one beside the fountain today, only me."

Mellicene did not know what to think. She felt that the boy was misleading her, but also could not altogether disbelieve him. She threatened to whip him if he were deceiving her, and she reported the incident to her lady, Guinevere. But Guinevere laughed and mocked at her, telling her she had been dreaming when she beheld that vision.

Mellicene Ran Down the Turret Stairs.

But on yet another morning Mellicene saw the knight again. This time she woke her mistress and Guinevere too saw the noble knight; but this time he had taken off his golden collar as he washed. Quickly they ran down the turret stairs to solve the mystery.

Once again, King Arthur heard them coming and quickly put on his magic cap. The Lady Guinevere marveled to see only the gardener's boy at the fountain and questioned him about the knight. Again Arthur told her that he was the only one who had been at the fountain that morning.

In his haste to put on his cap, King Arthur had forgotten about his golden collar. Suddenly Guinevere noticed it, shining in the sun.

"Do you mock me, boy?" she scoffed at King Arthur, "for how would a gardener's boy have a golden collar about his neck? I have a mind to have you whipped. But take that collar and return it to the knight to whom it belongs. Tell him a true knight does not hide in a lady's garden."

"Do You Mock Me, Boy?"

All that day as she sat over her embroidery, Guinevere marveled over the mystery and sought to solve it. Then she suddenly had an idea. She asked Mellicene to have the gardener's boy come inside, bringing a basket of roses.

When King Arthur entered the lady's chamber, her attendants cried out at his rudeness.

"Take your cap off in the lady's presence," they demanded.

"I cannot," answered Arthur.

"I bid you take off your cap at once!" Guinevere ordered.

"I cannot take it off, because I have an ugly sore on my head," said Arthur.

"Then wear it," said Guinevere, but as he brought the roses to her, she suddenly snatched at the cap and plucked it off his head.

King Arthur was immediately transformed into his own self. He let fall the basket of roses which scattered all over the floor. Some of Guinevere,s attendants shrieked in terror, but Guinevere herself remained calm. She recognized him

"Take Off Your Cap in the Lady's Presence!"

as the wounded knight she had seen in the hermit's cell.

Guinevere laughed mockingly and flung King Arthur's cap back at him.

"Take your cap," she said, "gardener's boy who has an ugly sore on his head."

Arthur did not reply, but with as much dignity as possible replaced the cap on his head and was once more the gardener's boy. He turned and left, leaving the roses scattered on the floor.

From that time forward, whenever Guinevere saw him she would make sport of him and his "ugly sore". But privately she told her attendants not to mention this mystery to anyone else at the court.

She Recognizes the Wounded Knight.

Bad Times Came to Cameliard.

CHAPTER 11

King Arthur Challenges
Duke Mordaunt

Then bad times came to the Kingdom of Cameliard. King Ryence of North Wales and Duke Mordaunt lay siege, once more demanding the return of land and Guinevere's hand in marriage. Each day Duke Mordaunt paraded in front of the castle on horseback, challenging any knight of Cameliard to meet him. Yet he was such a fierce knight, known for his strength and violence, that no one dared to take up his challenge. King Leode-grance listened to his boasts with shame and sorrow.

All this while, Arthur, digging in the king's

garden, was aware of everything that was occurring. Finally he could not bear the affront to his lady any longer. He laid aside his spade, and through a back way traveled into the town. He took off his magic cap and found his way to the house of a rich merchant, Ralph of Cardiff. King Arthur showed the merchant his golden collar and his undergarments of fine purple silk, embroidered with gold.

"Sir merchant," he said, "you have heard of the insults the Lady Guinevere and the people of Cameliard have received from the Duke Mordaunt. I am a noble knight who dares to take up the duke's challenge. But I have no armor. I will pledge these possessions to you for a worthy suit of armor. I give my knightly word that if I do not pay you for the armor after a time, you may have this golden collar and these fine clothes."

The merchant saw that Arthur was no ordinary knight errant and soon agreed. He found for Arthur the best armor available, for he too longed for the defeat of the arrogant Duke Mordaunt.

"I Dare to Take Up the Challenge."

He thanked her for her boon and with an uplifted and joyous heart rode out to do battle with Duke Mordaunt.

Now the report had gone throughout Cameliard that a knight was to go forth to fight the duke. Great crowds gathered upon the walls, and King Leodegrance and the Lady Guinevere came to where the castle wall overlooked the meadow defended by Duke Mordaunt.

Suddenly the gates of the castle were lifted up and the knight of the White Shield rode forth. The hoofs of his war-horse thundered and his armor flamed like lightning. A great shout of approval went up from the people of Cameliard.

When Duke Mordaunt saw a knight clad in white, he rode directly to him and spoke words of knightly greeting.

"Sir, I see that you bear no crest upon your shield, so I do not know who you are. Yet I believe that only a knight of good quality would dare challenge me."

"What Token Would You Like?"

"Sir Knight," answered King Arthur, "I am of quality equal to your own. And as for my courage, I believe I have fought as many noble battles as you."

"Make your prayers then," scoffed Duke Mordaunt, "for I have defeated better men than you."

To this taunt King Arthur answered calmly, "That shall be according to the will of Heaven, Sir Knight, and not to your own."

With that the two champions saluted each other and rode to their assigned stations. Each gripped his spear and shield and made ready for the great encounter. A wonderful silence fell upon the crowd in anticipation of the battle. Then, all of a sudden, each shouted to his war-horse and launched forth. And so they met in the midst of the course with a noise like thunder. The spear of Duke Mordaunt burst into splinters, but King Arthur's spear did not, so the duke was cast out of his saddle and spun around like a windmill, whirling in the air before he finally fell to earth.

"I Have Defeated Better Men Than You."

Then he rolled over three times and lay absolutely still. His friends feared he was dead, but he recovered after a few hours.

King Arthur sat quietly on his horse. Then he quickly rode off to the forest, an unknown champion who had saved his lady.

The Duke was Cast Out of His Saddle.

King Arthur Joyous in His Victory

CHAPTER 12

The White Knight Returns

King Arthur, joyous in his victory, rode forth to seek the knights of his court who had ridden with him to Tintagolon. But meanwhile, Duke Mordaunt recovered from his wounds and plotted against King Leodegrance once more. "Surely the White Knight is gone, and no new challenger in Cameliard can defeat me," he thought.

He rode to the walls of the castle and called out a challenge to King Leodegrance.

"I make you a fair offer. Tomorrow I ride out in the meadow with six of my most noble knights. If you can find seven knights to take up our challenge and defeat us, I will renounce all claim to the Lady Guinevere. But if you cannot, then not only will you give me the lady to wed, but you will hand over to me three of the best castles in your possession." With that his herald blew his trumpet and off rode the duke.

King Leodegrance was in despair, for the White Knight had disappeared for two days, and Leodegrance knew of no one else who could help him. He went straight to his chamber and shut himself inside, for the marriage of his daughter to Duke Mordaunt was a thought he could not bear.

Meanwhile, word reached Arthur and his knights of the duke's new challenge. So together with his nephew, Sir Gawaine, and three other brave knights, Sir Geraint, Sir Ewaine, and Sir Pelias, King Arthur rushed back toward Cameliard.

On the day of the challenge, the morning passed and part of the afternoon, and still no knights faced Duke Mordaunt and his

"If You Can Find Seven Knights . . ."

companions. Then suddenly in the distance appeared a cloud of dust. And out of that dust came the five champions, riding at great speed. The people of the town recognized Sir Gawaine, Sir Ewaine, Sir Geraint and Sir Pelias, for they were knights of great renown. Leading them was the White Knight who had returned in their time of need.

Duke Mordaunt arrogantly addressed the White Knight.

"Several days ago I condescended to fight you, and you were lucky enough to unhorse me. But this is a more serious quarrel. I will not fight you unless you tell me who you are and what your rank is. Besides we cannot fairly fight you as we are seven and you are five."

King Arthur would not answer, but Sir Gawaine lifted his helmet and replied.

"Be aware, Duke Mordaunt, that I am at least of equal condition and estate as you, and the White Knight is above me. You should be honored to contest against him. And as to seven against

Suddenly Appeared a Cloud of Dust.

five, the odds are equal when you compare your valor to ours."

At the sound of these words, Duke Mordaunt turned red and made ready for battle. A great hush fell on the crowd as the combatants turned to face each other. But in the first pass, King Arthur and his knights unseated three knights. Included among them was Duke Mordaunt, who was defeated by the White Knight. The strength of the White Knight's spear blow was so severe that Duke Mordaunt was instantly killed.

Arthur then turned to his knights and said: "My battle is done for the day. Now they are four and you are four. I will watch the valor of my knights from afar."

With that, his knights returned to the lists and easily overcame the knights from North Umber, who had lost all will to fight after Mordaunt's death. A great shout went up from the people of Cameliard, and they opened the gates to welcome their heroes. But while King Arthur's knights

"My Battle is Done for the Day."

entered the gates, the White Knight himself was nowhere to be seen.

For the next few days, King Leodegrance entertained his guests and thanked them for their assistance. Everyone in Cameliard was happy and felt sure that peace had finally come. No one paid any attention to the re-appearance of the gardener's boy who always wore a cap.

But then a herald from King Ryence appeared boldly before King Leodegrance. The herald informed him that King Ryence was greatly displeased by the fate of Duke Mordaunt and re-issued his challenge for certain territories. Unless those territories were handed over, King Ryence would attack Cameliard with a large army.

Once again King Leodegrance was plunged into despair. Once again he wondered where he could find the White Knight who had already rescued his kingdom twice.

He called his daughter before him, because he had noticed that the White Knight seemed to

King Ryence Was Greatly Displeased.

have special regard for her.

"My daughter," he said, "do you know how to summon the White Knight? We need his help, for our enemy King Ryence is threatening at our doors."

"You had sooner ask the gardener's boy about the White Knight than me," answered Guinevere.

"Foolish girl, do you jest when the kingdom is in danger?" shouted her father.

"Nay father, I do not jest. For I have noticed that whenever the White Knight is present, that boy is missing, and whenever that boy is here, the White Knight cannot be found."

The king at once ordered the boy to be sent to him. When he appeared he was wearing his cap.

"Take off your cap in my presence," demanded the king.

"I cannot take off my cap," King Arthur answered.

But then Lady Guinevere, who stood beside the chair of King Leodegrance, spoke up. "I do

"You Had Sooner Ask the Gardener's Boy."

beseech you, for my sake, take off your cap."

At these words, he took off his cap, and King Leodegrance immediately recognized him. He knelt before him, took Arthur's hands in his and said, "My lord, my lord, is it you who has performed these wondrous deeds?"

Guinevere was astonished beyond measure. She had thought that Arthur was of noble blood, but did not realize he was the king of the realm.

Arthur noticed that Guinevere had turned pale and addressed her softly. "Lady, what cheer?"

"I am afraid of your greatness," answered Guinevere.

"Nay lady, rather it is I who am afraid of you," said Arthur. "For I love you so deeply that whether or not you have feelings for me is my deepest concern. Do you have feelings for me?"

"I do, my lord", said Guinevere softly.

"Do you have strong feelings for me?" asked Arthur.

"Yes, I do," smiled Guinevere.

Then Arthur bent his head and kissed his lady

"For My Sake, Take Off Your Cap."

before all who were present. There and then they became engaged to be married.

Shortly afterwards King Arthur led his army to victory against King Ryence. He then looked forward to his marriage to Guinevere and bringing her to his court as his queen.

"Do You Have Strong Feelings For Me?"

The Streets Were Strewn with Flowers.

CHAPTER 13

The Round Table Established

In the early fall of the year, King Arthur, at his court in Camelot, prepared for the arrival of his bride. In readiness for the wedding, the cobblestone streets were strewn with flowers. All along the way the royal couple would pass hung tapestries of gold and crimson. Everywhere flags and pennants floated in the warm gentle breeze.

King Arthur eagerly awaited the arrival of the Lady Guinevere and her court, and at last the herald announced them. King Arthur and his court of knights brought King Leodegrance and Lady Guinevere with great ceremony into

Camelot and the royal castle, while all around the townspeople cheered lustily. And when high noon came, the entire court went with great pomp and majesty into the cathedral, and there the two noble souls were married by the archbishop.

The bells of the city rang out joyfully and all the people outside the cathedral shouted acclaim. For Arthur was beloved by his people and all were happy in his happiness. What followed was the most magnificent wedding feast ever, and all marveled at the courtliness of Arthur and the beauty of Guinevere.

This day also became famous in the annals of chivalry. For on this day the Round Table was established, which was the very flower and the chief glory of Arthur's reign.

In the middle of the afternoon, Arthur and his court entered a splendid pavilion that Merlin had built with magic. The walls were painted with wonderful figures of saints and angels.

Overhead the roof depicted the sky and the

The Two Noble Souls Were Married.

stars, and in the midst of the sky was an image of the sun. The floor was a pavement of marble stones, set in squares of black, white, blue, red and other colors.

The center of the room held the Round Table with seats for exactly fifty knights. At each place was a gold plate filled with bread, and a gold chalice filled with wine. When the king and his court entered, suddenly music was heard, but there were no musicians seen.

Merlin took Arthur by the hand and led him to the center. "Here," he said, "behold the Round Table."

Merlin showed the king the various marvels of the Round Table. First he pointed out a special high seat, wrought in precious woods. This was the royal seat for Arthur himself. And as Merlin spoke, suddenly on the back of the seat in gold letters appeared the words

ARTHUR, KING

Opposite the royal seat, Merlin told Arthur, was the Seat Perilous. Only one man in all the

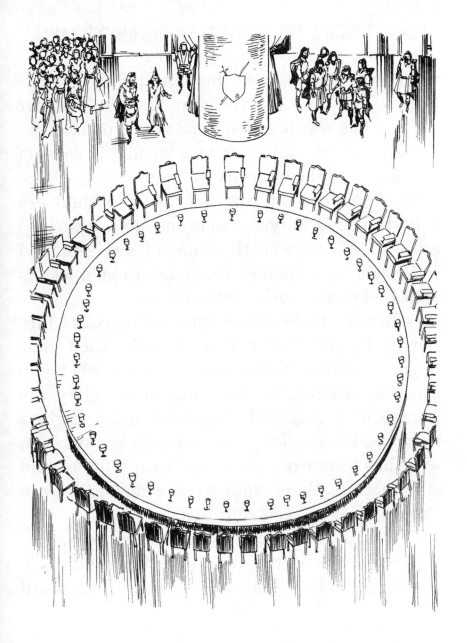

The Round Table

world was worthy to sit there. And if anyone unworthy tried to take the seat, he would suffer death. Thus was it called the Seat Perilous.

"Merlin," asked Arthur, "can we fill the seats of the Round Table with fifty knights?"

"No," answered Merlin, "for right now there are only thirty-two knights noble enough to sit here." And Merlin called off the name of each one, and as he said their names, the words in gold letters appeared on the backs of the seats.

"When the table is complete and there are fifty worthy knights," Merlin continued, "then your reign will start to fall into disorder. For when any man has reached the crowning of his glory, his work is done and God shatters him. So might a man break a chalice from which so wonderful a wine has been drunk that no lesser wine should ever touch it. When your work is done, God will shatter the chalice of your life."

The king looked calmly at Merlin and said, "Old man, your words are always filled with wisdom and wonder. Whatever fate befalls me, I will

"Only Thirty-Two Knights Noble Enough..."

work for God's purposes."

Thus was the Round Table established with great pomp and ceremony. The Archbishop of Canterbury blessed each and every seat and each chosen knight took his place at the table. All those who stood near the place, both knights and ladies, lifted up their voices in loud acclaim.

Then all the knights arose and each knight held up before him the cross of the hilt of his sword. Each knight repeated word for word the oath that King Arthur spoke, for this was the covenant of their knighthood.

They would be gentle to the weak, courageous to the strong, and terrible to the wicked. They swore to defend the helpless who called upon them for aid. They would hold all women sacred, and they would defend one another in any way they were asked. They were to be merciful to all men, gentle of deed, true in friendship, and faithful in love. Each knight swore to the covenant and then kissed the hilt of his sword. All who heard their oaths shouted once more in acclaim.

Then All the Knights Arose.

Then all the knights of the Round Table seated themselves. They broke bread and poured wine, giving thanks to God for what they ate and drank and for eternal brotherhood.

Thus was King Arthur married to Guinevere and the Round Table established.

Giving Thanks for Eternal Brotherhood

Queen Morgana Le Fay

CHAPTER 14

Queen Morgana's Anger

Queen Morgana le Fay, King Arthur's stepsister, was a cunning enchantress. She was the mistress of so much magic that with her potent spells she could work her will on all things. In earlier years she had been the pupil of Merlin, and next to him she was the most powerful magician in the world. But unlike Merlin she had no gift for prophecy.

Lately Queen Morgana had grown angry with King Arthur for what she perceived as a slight. Her son, Sir Baudemagus, had not been deemed worthy to become a member of the Round Table. Queen Morgana grew more and more bitter for this affront, and felt she could have no pleasure in life unless she punished Arthur.

But Queen Morgana was aware that she could never do her brother an injury as long as Merlin was there to protect him. She knew that to destroy the king she would have to destroy Merlin first.

At her court lived a young girl of marvelous and bewitching beauty. She was of royal blood, being the daughter of the King of Northumberland. Her name was Vivien. Vivien was wise and cunning beyond her years. But she had no heart and was cold and cruel inside. Queen Morgana liked her and taught her all the magic and sorcery she knew. Yet Vivien did not feel any love toward her mistress.

One day Vivien and Morgana sat together in a garden in Avalon, Queen Morgana's country, looking out over the beautiful ocean. Finally, Morgana asked Vivien "What, do you desire more than anything else in the world?"

Wise and Cunning, But Cold and Cruel

"Lady, I would most want the wisdom you have, more than anything else," answered Vivien.

Queen Morgana laughed and continued, "It is possible for you to become as wise as I am, and even wiser too, if you will follow my orders. For I know a way in which you may obtain that wisdom."

Vivien pressed her, and the queen went on. "Listen and I will tell. You must know Merlin, whom you have seen several times at the court of King Arthur. He is the master of all the wisdom that it is possible for anyone to possess in this world. All that I know of magic, Merlin has taught me. And he knows many things that he has not taught me. Merlin taught me when I was young, because I was beautiful and caught his eye. For Merlin loves female beauty above all things in this world, and so he taught me magic and was most patient with me.

"But Merlin has a gift which belongs to him

"All I Know of Magic, Merlin Has Taught Me."

alone and which he cannot communicate to anyone else, for it is instinct with him. That is the gift of seeing into the future.

"Yet though he can foresee the fate of others, he is blind to his own. He confessed this to me several times. Now Vivien, you are even more beautiful than I was at your age, and besides I will give you a certain charm that will make you irresistible to Merlin. He will love you so much that he will impart more wisdom to you than he did to me.

"But you must know, as your beauty fades, he may regret imparting this wisdom to you and may lay a spell upon you to deprive you of your powers. For the world cannot hold two people who know so much magic."

Vivien listened with a great deal of attention, and when Queen Morgana had ended, she said, "Dear lady, all that you tell me is wonderful, and I want to know all Merlin's secrets. If you will help me in this matter, I will be forever in your

"The World Cannot Hold Two Like Us."

debt. And do not worry about the danger involved. For I will use the knowledge Merlin gives me to cast a spell upon him, and he shall never again be able to harm me or anyone else. I shall play my wit against his wisdom, my beauty against his cunning, and I believe I shall win this game."

Queen Morgana laughed so hard she could not stop. "Certainly, Vivien, you are cunning beyond your years. Whoever could suppose so young a girl could bring about the downfall of the world's wisest magician?"

With that, she put a thin whistle to her lips and blew. Servants came in carrying a casket of alabaster filled with precious stones. Morgana took out two rings, one with a clear white stone, the other with a bright red one.

"Vivien," she said, "look at these two rings. They each possess a spell of incredible potency. For if you wear the ring with the white stone, whoever wears the ring with the red stone will love you with a passion so strong that he will do

A Casket Filled With Precious Stones

whatever you want. Take your rings to King Arthur's court and use your cunning to bring down Merlin."

Vivien took the two rings and gave Queen Morgana thanks beyond measure.

Vivien Took the Two Rings.

The Dwarf Bore a Cushion With a Ring.

CHAPTER 15

Merlin and Vivien

King Arthur took great pleasure in holding a grand feast each Pentecost, at which time his court gathered around him for mirth, good cheer, and entertainment. As all the nobles sat at the feast, into the hall suddenly came a beautiful maiden and a hideous dwarf. The maiden was dressed in flame-colored satin, her hair was red, and her eyes shone black. The dwarf was also clad in red and bore in his hands a cushion of flame-colored silk with tassels of gold. Upon the cushion was a ring of great beauty set with a red stone.

King Arthur thought he recognized the maiden and asked her who she was.

"I am the daughter of the King of Northumberland, and my name is Vivien," she answered.

Then King Arthur asked her what she had on the cushion and why she brought it to the feast.

"Lord, I have very good entertainment for Pentecost. For here is a ring of such a sort that only he who is the most wise and worthy of all men may wear it."

"Let us see this ring," said King Arthur.

Vivien took the ring from the cushion and brought it to King Arthur. The king took the ring into his own hands and asked to try it on. But when he tried to place the ring on his finger, it shrank in size so that it could not pass beyond the first joint.

"It appears that I am not worthy to wear this ring," he laughed.

"My lord," asked Vivien, "do I have leave to have others in your court try on the ring?"

"Let Us See This Ring."

King Arthur agreed. Various members of the court tried on the ring, but it fit no one. Then Vivien came to the place where Merlin sat. She kneeled before him and offered him the ring. And as Merlin could not foresee his own future, he saw no harm intended to him. "Child, what is this silly trick you offer me?"

"Sir," answered Vivien, "I beg you to try this ring upon your finger."

Merlin looked at her closely and was attracted to her great beauty. He said more gently to her, "Why should I take the ring?"

"Because I believe you are the most wise and worthy man in this place, and the ring belongs to you," Vivien answered.

Merlin smiled and took the ring and placed it upon his finger. It fit exactly. Vivien cried out, "See, the ring fits!"

Merlin was pleased at first. But when he wanted to take it off, he could not, for the ring had attached itself to his finger as if it were of his flesh and bones. Merlin became troubled about

"What is This Silly Trick?"

the magic in the ring.

"Lady," he asked, "where came you by this ring?"

"Sir," answered Vivien, "you know all things. Why do you not know that this ring was sent here by Morgana le Fay?"

Merlin grew more worried and said, "I hope there is no evil in this ring."

Vivien smiled upon him and answered, "What evil could there be in it?"

By this time the great magic in the ring had begun to work upon Merlin's spirit. He took more and more pleasure in Vivien's beauty. Soon his passion was so great it was as if his heart was pierced with violent agony.

Vivien saw the ring's power and laughed and turned away. Several others observed the strange manner in which Merlin regarded her, but accounted it only to Vivien's great beauty.

After some time the enchantment of the ring grew so strong that Merlin could not disentangle himself from Vivien's witchcraft. Wherever she

"Where Came You By This Ring?"

went, he followed. And all the court made merry and jested at the old man following the young girl. Vivien hated Merlin with all her heart, and he wearied her with his regard. But she pretended to have a great affection for him.

Now one day as she sat in the garden, Merlin followed her. She rose in haste to escape him, but Merlin hurried and overtook her.

"Child," he asked, "do you then hate me?"

"Sir, I do not hate you," answered Vivien.

But Merlin did not believe her.

"What can I do for you to make you love me?" he asked.

Quickly Vivien answered, "If you would impart to me your great wisdom and cunning, I believe I could love you."

Merlin looked steadily at Vivien and realized she was not as innocent as she looked. Yet still his love for her was so great that he promised to teach her all the magic he knew.

Shortly after, Vivien asked King Arthur for leave to visit her father in Northumberland.

"I Believe I Could Love You."

King Arthur agreed, and Merlin left with her. But they did not go to Northumberland. For Merlin had agreed to teach her his magic in a private place.

Merlin Agreed to Teach Her His Magic.

"How Will He Provide Shelter?"

CHAPTER 16

Merlin's Fate

Merlin, Vivien, and their attendants travelled deep into a lonely woods. It was a desolate place, and Merlin's followers grew worried.

"The enchanter has brought us here, but how will he provide shelter for the change in seasons?"

Merlin overheard their whispers and assured them they would soon find a good resting place. Then he told them to stand a distance away while he conjured. Merlin recited a powerful spell, and before their very eyes appeared shapes and forms that rose high into the air. Then a cloud of red dust covered their eyes. When the dust cleared, they saw a marvellous castle which glowed in the moonlight.

When Vivien saw what Merlin had done, she kneeled before him, took his hand in hers and kissed it.

"Master," she said, "will you teach me how to do this?"

"I will teach you how to do this and much more besides. I will teach you how to transform shapes. I will teach you spells and charms that no man has ever heard before."

"You are the most wonderful man in the world," Vivien cried out.

"You don't hate me any more?" asked Merlin.

"No, master," she answered.

But she lied, for in her heart she was evil and the heart of Merlin was good. That which is evil will always hate that which is good. While Vivien spoke lovingly to Merlin, inside she hated and feared him. For she knew that without the magic ring, he would come to see her for what she really was. As soon as Merlin has taught me all he

Evil Will Always Hate Good.

knows, the world will be too small for both of us, she thought, and I will destroy him.

Merlin and Vivien lived together in that place for a little more than a year. He taught her all of the magic he was able to impart. At the end of that time he said to her, "Vivien, I have now taught you so much that I believe there is no one in all of the world who knows more magic than you do."

Vivien was filled with great joy. And she said in her heart, "Now Merlin, if I have good fortune enough to entangle you in my spells, you shall never see the world again."

On the next day Vivien called for a feast to be prepared for herself and Merlin. By the means of the knowledge she had gained from Merlin she secretly prepared a very powerful sleeping potion which she poured into Merlin's wine glass.

When the feast was over, Vivien came to Merlin and said:

The World Will Be Too Small for Both of Us.

"Take this chalice and drink the wine within it. For the wine is noble and so are you." Then she set her lips to the chalice and kissed it, but did not really drink from it. Merlin suspected no evil and gulped the wine with great cheerfulness.

After a little the fumes of the sleeping potion began to effect him and Merlin realized he had been tricked.

"Help! Help!" he cried out in agony. "I have been betrayed!"

He tried to get up but fell backwards.

Vivien sat with her chin upon her hands and regarded him steadily, smiling strangely at him. When Merlin fell into a deep sleep, Vivien wove a powerful spell around him that bound him in a web of enchantment. And Merlin was like an insect caught in a silver spider's web.

The next morning when Merlin awoke from his sleep he saw Vivien looking at him, but he could not move.

"Behold, Merlin, you are altogether in my power. You cannot move a single hair without my

"I Have Been Betrayed!"

will. And now I will leave you, and go into the world. All your power and magic will pass to me."

Vivien struck her hands together and summoned her attendants. She presented Merlin before them, and made them pluck his beard and pinch his arms and hands, but Merlin could do nothing. They all laughed at Merlin and mocked him. Then Vivien used her magic to create a great coffin of stones. She had Merlin lifted on the coffin and then placed a huge stone slab upon it.

Vivien used her magic to make the castle disappear and created a mist that no human eye could ever penetrate. And Merlin was never seen nor heard from again.

"You are Altogether in My Power."

Sir Launcelot

CHAPTER 17

Sir Launcelot and Queen Guinevere

Of all the knights of the Round Table the greatest was Sir Launcelot. He was known for his valor, his courage, and his manly beauty. No knight performed more difficult deeds, no knight rescued more ladies, and no knight defended the weak as well as Sir Launcelot. Because of his great character and great goodness, King Arthur loved and trusted him most of all his knights.

Sir Launcelot was a special friend of Queen Guinevere. From his earliest appearance at Camelot he pledged her his loyalty, and all the deeds he performed were in her honor. The queen admired Sir Launcelot and loved to hear him tell stories and sing and dance. He would accompany her on trips and often visit her private bower.

Now ugly rumors began to circulate that the queen and Sir Launcelot were more than friends. And after a time, the rumors began to reach the ears of the king. At first he paid no attention. But as the rumors persisted, he grew cold toward his wife and his trust in Sir Launcelot grew weaker.

These rumors were fueled by members of the court who were envious of Sir Launcelot. Among those was Sir Modred, King Arthur's nephew, who aspired to the throne.

One night, Sir Modred called a page of the queen's court and said, "Go to Sir Launcelot, and tell him the queen wishes to speak to him." The page delivered his message, and Sir Launcelot, suspecting no evil, went secretly to the queen's apartment.

Guinevere was surprised to see him, and

"Go to Sir Launcelot."

Launcelot grew immediately suspicious, for he knew he had enemies at the court. Meanwhile Sir Modred watched at the entrance to the queen's apartment until he saw Sir Launcelot enter. Then he ran to his brother, Sir Agravaine, and told him that Sir Launcelot was in the queen's private chamber, betraying the king. Sir Agravaine gathered together eleven knights and rushed to the queen's apartment to arrest Sir Launcelot.

But the lady attendants of the queen saw the knights rushing toward her chamber and alerted Guinevere and Launcelot to the plot against them. They locked the doors to protect themselves.

Sir Agravaine knocked and cried aloud in a thunderous voice:

"You traitor knight! What is your business here behind the queen's locked doors? Come forth to us, your fellows of the Round Table, and explain."

Sir Launcelot looked around the queen's

"You Traitor Knight!"

chamber for a suit of armor to protect himself, but found none.

"Lady, I must open the door and fight them without armor," he told Guinevere. "But if I perish, you must go to my relatives and ask asylum. For you will no longer receive justice at this court. What was once the fairest place on earth is now beset with treachery and suspicion."

By this time, Sir Agravaine, Sir Modred and their allies had taken a battering ram and were trying to break down the doors. But Sir Launcelot opened the door just a crack, enough to allow one knight, Sir Colgrance of Gore, to enter. This knight, seeing Launcelot without armor, struck him a fierce blow with his sword. But Launcelot dodged the blow and with his own sword struck down Sir Colgrance and quickly bolted the door.

"My queen," he called out, "help me into this armor. Then can I make my escape."

Sir Launcelot put on the armor, opened the door and like a wild man took on the group of

At the Queen's Doors

knights who had come to attack him.

Straight away he killed Sir Agravaine, and in the fighting killed seven other knights including Sir Florence and Sir Lovel, the young sons of Sir Gawaine. He wounded Sir Modred, who made his escape.

Sir Launcelot turned to Queen Guinevere and cried aloud:

"My lady, I must leave this place for ever, for tonight I have killed the nephew of the king and two of the sons of my dear friend, Sir Gawaine. But I will not desert you, because they will come to try you for treason tomorrow. I will leave now and gather knights loyal to me and come to your rescue."

The queen fell weeping on her bed and cried. "Alas, alas, the end of the kingdom is approaching."

Straight Away He Killed Sir Agravine.

Modred Finds the King.

CHAPTER 18

A Daring Escape

Sir Modred had his wound bound up and rode to the inn where King Arthur was staying. When King Arthur saw his nephew all bandaged, he asked him what had happened. Modred explained that Sir Launcelot had been caught in the queen's private chamber and when asked to surrender had killed, among others, the king's nephew, Sir Agravaine, and the two young sons of Sir Gawaine before he had made his escape.

The king groaned aloud and declared that tomorrow the queen would be tried for treason. Then ne went to a private place to grieve.

"Alas, all is as Merlin said it would be," he said to himself. "All my realm reels back into savagery and the end approaches."

Then he ordered the queen brought to trial in a plain robe and barefoot. "For I shall not believe her to be innocent until she is proved so," he sighed.

When the queen heard that she was to be dressed as a common criminal she wept bitterly "My lord, the king, has already condemned me in his heart," she cried, "so that my trial will mean my death!"

Word of the trial reached Sir Launcelot. He had gathered together the knights of the Round Table loyal to him, including Sir Bors and Sir Lionel.

As the queen was led barefoot to her trial, Sir Launcelot hastened to her rescue. For the first time knights of the Round Table fought each other in deadly combat. Sir Launcelot, in the fury of battle, struck and killed Sir Gareth and Sir Geharis, two of his dearest comrades-in-arms.

Dressed as a Common Criminal

Finally, Sir Launcelot reached the queen. He cut her ropes and placed her on the saddle of his own horse.

"Let us escape, while there is still time!" he called to his men. So together with the queen and the knights still loyal to him, Sir Launcelot made his way to his castle, Joyous Gard, where he offered the queen peace and asylum.

Meanwhile, in the battle, twenty-seven knights of the king and sixteen of Sir Launcelot's party were killed. Included was King Arthur's old friend, Sir Kay. As Arthur looked down at the body of his old friend, he saw another sign that the kingdom was nearing its end.

The daring moves made by Sir Launcelot could be called the beginning of the end of King Arthur's reign. Sir Launcelot stepped between the law and the queen, because he felt bound by his honor to cherish and protect her. But King Arthur was equally bound to recover his queen and punish her as a lawbreaker. That she had

"Let Us Escape!"

gone off with Sir Launcelot was an act the king could never condone or forgive.

When the news of the battle reached King Arthur, he was filled with anger and grief.

"The joy of the Round Table is gone to grief," he said, "and it shall never be the same again." Merlin's prophecy once more would be fulfilled.

By now Sir Gawaine had sworn undying hatred to Sir Launcelot and counseled King Arthur to attack Joyous Gard. But Arthur hesitated, not from cowardice, but because he had no wish to attack his own knights of the Round Table who had sided with Sir Launcelot. Reluctantly he summoned all his remaining knights together and ordered the attack.

Sir Launcelot and his brother Sir Ector stood on the parapets of Joyous Gard and watched the great army of King Arthur as it marched towards them.

"Would it not be better to compromise with the king and return his queen to him?" Sir Ector asked his brother.

Arthur Orders the Attack.

"Never," returned Sir Launcelot, "until the king can insure her safety. It would bring great dishonor to us."

And so the war went on.

It Would Bring Great Dishonor to Us.

Assault on Joyous Gard

CHAPTER 19

The Siege of Joyous Gard

The army of King Arthur made assault upon assault on the castle of Joyous Gard. They made breaches in the walls. But these breaches were rebuilt at night. Each side lost many men and both armies suffered dreadfully.

The counselors to Sir Launcelot decided it was time to make a break through the king's lines and seek the sea so that they could journey to France and safety. Sir Launcelot tried one last time to make peace between himself and Arthur.

That afternoon he appeared upon the bat tle-ments of his castle and asked to speak to King Arthur. Arthur's troops thought perhaps Sir

Launcelot was going to surrender so they ran to the king. King Arthur hurried to ask Launcelot if he would indeed surrender.

"I would speak to you of other things," said Sir Launcelot. "Why are you assaulting this castle? Inside are many brave knights of the Round Table. Is it to your honor to kill these worthy, honorable knights?"

"You forget, sir," called King Arthur, "that you have unlawfully seized my queen. Surrender her to me and we can talk further."

"Your queen is held in high honor here, safe from injury. Pledge her safety to me and I will surrender her to you."

"Am I to make a treaty for the return of my wife?" asked Arthur disdainfully.

Sir Gawaine also spoke. "Sir, you have forgotten you killed two of my brothers and two of my sons. There will never be peace between us!"

"Then God pity us for our un-Christian hatred," called Sir Launcelot and turned away.

"Is It to Your Honor?"

Thus it was decided in the castle to prepare for battle and escape. All of a sudden the walls to the castle were thrown open and Launcelot and his men burst forth in their daring attempt to break through the king's lines.

At first the charge seemed successful, but then Launcelot saw they were lost and their retreat would be cut off quickly.

"Retreat! retreat!" he called and together he and the queen barely made it back into the castle. Many lost their lives in the attempt, including Launcelot's dear friend, Sir Lionel. The cost of the war grew deeper and deeper.

The Bishop of Rochester came to the camp of King Arthur to try to make peace between the warring parties.

"Lord," he entreated, "let this quarrel between you and Sir Launcelot cease. Let there be peace once more in the land. For friend fights against friend, and brother fights against brother. What pleasure or honor can come from such a war?"

"The war was not of my forming," answered the

The Walls to the Castle Were Thrown Open.

king. "It was Sir Launcelot's fault. He and his fellows took my queen. Let them deliver the queen and there will be peace."

"They will not deliver the queen unless you declare upon your honor that no harm shall befall her."

Then the king sat with his fist on his forehead and thought about what the bishop had said.

Finally, in a broken voice he said to the bishop, "Let the queen be delivered to me at Camelot and I promise no harm shall be done to threaten or deprive her of her life."

"Let me have that in writing," said the bishop. King Arthur called for a scribe and wrote those words and handed them to the bishop, who hurried off to Joyous Gard.

The queen looked over the documents and was satisfied on her own behalf, but worried about all the knights that had remained loyal to her. Nothing was said of them in the document.

The bishop returned to Arthur with those concerns.

"Let the Queen be Delivered to Me."

"What other conditions do they impose upon me? Why should I pledge to those who have acted treasonably against me?" But then Sir Gawaine whispered something to Arthur and the king turned to the bishop and said.

"Very well, take my word to these knights that I will do no harm to them while they are within the kingdom of England."

The Bishop conveyed the news to Sir Launcelot.

"Let the king return to Camelot, and within three days time I will return the queen to him."

Thus ended a sad and cruel war in which many brave knights lost their lives and the fellowship of the Round Table was forever broken.

"I Will Do Them No Harm."

On the Third Day they Brought the Queen.

CHAPTER 20

Sir Gawaine Challenges
Sir Launcelot

The king went to Camelot and on the third day the queen was brought to him. Sir Launcelot and Queen Guinevere, with olive branches, symbols of peace, on their heads, approached the throne and knelt.

"King Arthur," said Sir Launcelot, "I return to you your queen. For thirteen weeks she has dwelt in my castle with the highest honor. I return her to you as pure as when you first saw her in Cameliard."

King Arthur frowned. For a while he said nothing and then finally spoke:

"Sir, you were once my friend and the best-beloved of all my knights. But that time is past, never to return. You took my queen by force for several months. Through your actions many brave knights have died. Yet now you stand before me and urge me to accept my queen with love and affection. That which has been undone must remain undone. The seat beside my throne will remain forever empty.

"Never again shall Queen Guinevere or any queen occupy it. Guinevere I renounce completely. I have pledged no harm will come to her, and herewith I give her over to the church where she shall remain a nun until the end of her days.

"As for you and your knights, I promised no harm would come to you on English soil. But from this moment forth you are hereby banished from this land forever and cannot return upon pain of death. And all your lands and properties shall be forfeit to the king."

Thus the queen was led away to an abbey, there

"You Took My Queen By Force."

to spend the rest of her days, and Sir Launcelot and his friends left for France, where they lived in sorrow and in sadness.

But still, even after they had departed, a rage burned inside Sir Gawaine, for he had sworn undying hatred of Sir Launcelot. Slowly he convinced King Arthur to attack Sir Launcelot in France. Arthur had agreed, Gawaine argued, not to attack Sir Launcelot in England. But he had the right to pursue him in France. Sir Gawaine convinced the king, and Arthur gathered an army and set sail for France. He left his nephew, Sir Modred, in charge in England.

King Arthur and his troops besieged Sir Launcelot in his castle at Chillion. As before, many brave knights died in the struggle. But the walls of the castle held. Then Sir Gawaine decided that he wanted to challenge Sir Launcelot directly.

The next morning he paraded in front of the castle, daring Sir Launcelot to fight. But Sir Launcelot, who still had a great love for his old

The Queen was Led Away.

friend, refused. But each and every morning Sir Gawaine's taunts grew worse, and on the fourth morning Sir Launcelot came out to meet him.

Never before had such a fierce battle been joined. Sir Gawaine fought with the strength often men, but even so the superior skill of Sir Launcelot overcame him. And when Sir Gawaine's shield lowered, Sir Launcelot struck him a blow that pierced his armor and wounded him severely. When Launcelot asked Gawaine to forgive him, Gawaine refused, saying he would die his enemy.

They carried Sir Gawaine's wounded body to King Arthur's tent. There Arthur saw his dying nephew and groaned aloud. But Sir Gawaine suddenly spoke to him in a clear voice.

"My lord, now that I am about to die, it is as if a film has been lifted from my eyes and I can see clearly. Sir Launcelot was never your true enemy. It was Sir Modred who plotted against you both. Even now in England he usurps your

Launcelot Struck Him a Severe Blow.

throne and plots to kill you on your return." With these words, Sir Gawaine closed his eyes and died.

King Arthur wept at the loss of his noble kinsman, but vowed to take action against Sir Modred.

Sir Modred Plotted Against You Both.

On the Far Side, a Lone Wounded Figure

CHAPTER 21

The Last Battle

King Arthur made peace with Sir Launcelot and withdrew his army to England. But there, waiting for him at the cliffs of Dover, was Sir Modred and an army loyal to him. Yet Sir Modred could not prevent King Arthur's army from landing. They fought a fierce battle by the shore, brother against brother, friend against friend, until the sea ran red with blood.

But finally the forces of King Arthur were victorious, and the army of Sir Modred broke and fled. Late that night, the king, accompanied by Sir Bedevere, surveyed the battlefield. On the far side he saw a lone wounded figure, walking in the mist.

"Sir Bedevere," he cried out, "isn't that my nephew, the traitor Sir Modred? Give me your spear so I may vanquish him forever!"

"But sire," said Sir Bedevere, "that is a desperate man without friends or family. Do not challenge him for he can turn on you like a wounded beast in its rage."

But King Arthur said, "What is my life to me now that I have lost my wife, the love of my youth, and all these knights, the chief glory and pride of my reign? What have I to live for besides an empty throne?"

With these words he grabbed Sir Bedevere's spear and rode off to challenge his enemy. Sir Modred drew his sword and it flashed like white light in the darkness. He came forward to meet King Arthur, whirling his sword on high. But the king drove the point of his spear into Sir Modred with such force that the spear came out through his back. Sir Modred knew he had received his

"What is Life to Me Now?"

death wound. But with a strength almost super-human, spurred by revenge, he pushed himself up the length of the spear and struck the king such a fierce blow that his sword cut through King Arthur's helmet.

The king reeled upon his saddle, and Sir Bedevere quickly caught him and brought him to his tent. But when his helmet was unstrapped, Arthur knew he had received his final wound. In a calm voice he asked Sir Bedevere to take his sword, Excaliber, and throw it deep into the water of a nearby lake.

Sir Bedevere ran to follow his king's last command, but when he reached the lake shore and looked at Excaliber, he thought again. It seems a waste to throw this beautiful sword into the water. I will keep it for myself and tell the king I did what he wanted, Sir Bedevere decided.

When he returned, King Arthur asked him what happened to the sword.

"I beheld nothing but the waves beating upon the shore," said Sir Bedevere.

His Sword Cut Through Arthur's Helmet.

"What? Do you betray me on my deathbed? Go back again and throw the sword into the lake!"

Sir Bedevere begged forgiveness and once again returned to the lake shore. But once again he could not bring himself to throw the sword into the lake.

When he returned, King Arthur again asked him what happened to Excaliber.

"I saw the moon shining on high and nothing else," answered Sir Bedevere.

"Still you deny my last wishes," cried out Arthur.

"Forgive me," begged Sir Bedevere and for the third time took the sword to the lake. This time he hurled Excaliber as far as he could toward the center of the lake. To his amazement, an arm clad in white samite reached up from the lake, and as its hand grabbed the sword and pulled it smoothly into the lake. Excaliber was no more.

He raced back to tell King Arthur what had happened.

"You have done well, Sir Bedevere," said the

"Do You Betray Me on My Deathbed?"

king. "Now carry me to the shore for there is a boat that is waiting for me."

Sir Bedevere did as his king commanded. There waiting was a brass boat and in it was the Lady of the Lake, Nymue, who had come for Arthur.

When King Arthur was placed in the boat, Sir Bedevere wept.

"My king, you are dying and I will be all alone."

King Arthur opened his eyes and said:

"Know that I shall not die at this place. For the Lady of the Lake has come to take me to the valley of Avalon where I shall yet live for many years. But the day will come when I shall return to England. And with my return will come peace, and war shall be no more. Take back this message and farewell."

With these words the great King Arthur disappeared.

War Shall Be No More.